How to recognize
30 edible
mushrooms

The cover photograph is of the Horse Mushroom, which is a giant variety of the common Meadow Mushroom (described on pages 44-47).

International Standard Book No. 0-8120-790-5

American edition published in 1977 by
Barron's Educational Series, Inc.
113 Crossways Park Drive
Woodbury, New York 11797

How to recognize 30 edible mushrooms

by
ANTOINE DEVIGNES

JACQUES PÉPIN
consultant

Translated by
G. W. GELDART

BARRON'S
Woodbury, New York

Contents

If you **carefully observe all the special features** that we give for the 30 edible species selected, you ought not to go wrong. . . .

If, at any time, you have the slightest doubt in your mind—and just having a doubt can cause indigestion—do not eat the specimen you are worried about.

When you want to improve your knowledge, remember that you can obtain further information through the many books listed in the bibliography. You can also join the North American Mycological Association, 4245 Redinger Road, Portsmouth, Ohio 45662. There may be a local mycological society in your area as well.

HOW TO AVOID
COSTLY MISTAKES

Most mushroom books devote a fair amount of space to a scientific description of each species, especially the reproductive systems of each and the classifications suggested by specialists. This is information that could be of great interest to ordinary people, and there are many who find it fascinating. Some of us, however, at any rate when we first begin, would prefer to know how to recognize edible mushrooms without having to go into details about their biological mechanisms.

If you like walking in the woods and are attracted by mushrooms, then you will find in this book a description of about thirty different edible species that are most commonly found in our woods and fields. It is, in fact, essential if you want to avoid all risk of making a mistake, to limit your first efforts to a few well-defined types. We have chosen, however, a sufficient number of different families of mushrooms so that you will be able to find something for your basket on every expedition.

In each case we have highlighted the special features for identification purposes, leaving out anatomical peculiarities that do not immediately concern us. In cases where there is a probability, or even a possibility, of confusing one mushroom with another to be avoided, the differences between them are displayed in such a way that you have only to make a careful examination, not requiring any extensive botanical knowledge, and there will be no trouble.

As much as possible we have left out scientific terms but, since certain scientific words are in constant use by the specialists, they need explaining. It is useful to know the names given to different parts of a mushroom because it eliminates the need for long descriptions. We have included an illustrated glossary to explain these terms.

Lastly, each mushroom has its own flavor and its own consistency. A recipe designed to bring out the flavor of one mushroom might spoil the taste of another. Experience has shown that there are one or more ways of cooking mushrooms that people like best. The recipes we give are for the benefit of cooks who have not been at it for long. Of course the "cordon bleu" experts will have their personal ideas, and if you are an imaginative cook you will soon invent your own way. . . .

The mushroom hunter does not need to dress up in special clothes and buy technical equipment as do the fisherman or the mountaineer, but he or she will do well to wear sensible clothing.

As a rule, the best collecting time is in the morning when the damp air favors the appearance of mushrooms. Clothing should be warm therefore and waterproof, but lightweight. Actually, people become so absorbed in the hunt that often they do not notice that they have wandered miles from their starting point and the sun has become scorchingly hot. Or sometimes they care caught by a storm and have to run for shelter in freezing rain. So it is a good idea to wear walking shoes that are supple but tough enough to stand up to ankle-deep mud or the dry, rough ruts of forest tracks.

A firm, flat-bottomed basket is best for holding the crop without damage. Paper bags are useful for special specimens. Avoid using plastic bags because mushrooms decompose very rapidly in plastic bags and quickly become unhealthy. A detailed map and a compass can come in handy for those who know how to use them.

One cannot always identify a mushroom at first sight

You can see at a glance some of the features that are essential to determine before deciding which species to gather; other features do not show up immediately. Although the overall shape of the mushroom and its components may give a good indication on the spot, a closer look at further clues helps to confirm the identification. The color of the spores is a good indicator, for instance. The spores are that microscopic dust that is usually carried on the lower surface of very many mushrooms; you can collect them by cutting off the stem and placing the cap for some time on a sheet of white or colored paper. This is why you have to make a second examination of everything in your basket when you return home.

The appearance of a mushroom varies according to the species, but it also changes with the age of the specimen

A mushroom normally looks like a little pillar with a dome on the top, and that is why we call anything that looks like this "mushroom-shaped." But a mushroom can just as well look like a piece of coral, a sponge, a cup, or a ball.

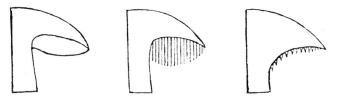

dome
and pillar

coral

sponge

cup

ball

In the first category, the dome—called the cap—is covered on its underside with vertical radiating gills or with vertical tubes or with spines.

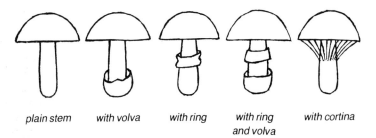

gills or flakes

tubes or pores

spines or teeth

The little pillar or stem, which supports the cap, may have a bag at the bottom end—the volva—or it may have a circular membrane around its middle—the ring—or it may have both at the same time. When the mushroom is young, the stem may also be joined to the cap by a cortina, a kind of veil that disappears with age leaving practically no trace of its presence.

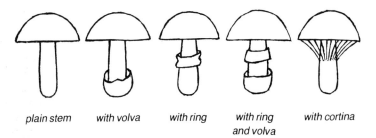

plain stem

with volva

with ring

with ring and volva

with cortina

The shape of the cap varies with the species and also with the age of the specimen. Often a young mushroom looks like an egg when it pushes up from the ground, and it is difficult to identify a species at this stage. After that it opens out and becomes depressed or curves inward; we can often find side by side mushrooms in the same family as a ball, a hemisphere, a flat disc, and a bowl.

The stem does not change as much as the cap. Whether it be slender or clublike, swollen at the base or cylindrical, quite plain or coming out of a volva, or with a ring, the stem keeps these features, short of some accident that might deform it. **We recommend carefully digging up the bottom end of a mushroom because this part is so necessary for correctly determining the species.**

Finally, the color is often a good guide for identification, especially the color of the gills. Nevertheless, if there are some species where there can be no doubt about the color, there are others that come in such a range of different shades that the beginner is quite puzzled.

> **It is only by observing all the special features that you can determine with certainty if a mushroom is to be thrown out or if it may be eaten without fear. There are no two species alike, and any mistake made comes from neglect in studying the distinguishing features.**

The tabulated description that we give for each of the species in this book will enable you to avoid making mistakes and proceed with confidence along the very pleasant road to enjoying wild mushrooms.

The real identification is made when you arrive home

When you arrive home you must examine again all the mushrooms one at a time, and identify them using the descriptions we provide, taking special care with those features that distinguish the species that look alike.

Before you start the identification, separate all the ones with a cap and stem from the other kinds. The first group then falls into three categories according to whether the mushrooms have pores, teeth, or gills underneath the cap. Mushrooms with tubes and teeth are sufficient indicators by themselves. Gills, on the other hand, have to be examined in combination with other parts connected with the stem. The following listing is a guide for identifying the mushrooms described in this book:

With ring only	type: Parasol (page 48)
With volva only	type: Sheathed Amanita (page 54)
With ring and volva	type: Caesars' Mushroom (page 50)
With cortina	type: Berkeley's Cortinarius (page 62)
Neither volva, nor ring, nor cortina	type: Russula and Lactarius (pages 30, 56)

Next take a specimen from each of these categories, preferably one that has opened out, and examine the spores. To collect them you should cut off the stem close to the cap and then place the cap with the gills in contact with a sheet of paper. Use a white paper if you think the spores will be black, brown, or yellow. You can usually guess this from the color of the gills. Use a darkly colored or black paper if you think the spores are white. After a few hours there will be enough spores on the paper for you to see what color they are.

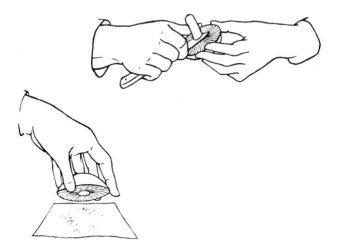

The answers to the following questions will provide preliminary classification for your mushrooms. They are set out in the order in which they should be asked:

What is the general shape of the mushroom?	What is there underneath the cap?	What sort of a stem does it have?	What color are the spores?
cap and stem	gills	plain with ring only with volva only with ring & volva with cortina	
	tubes spines		
sponge			
cup			
coral			
ball			

This preliminary sorting will make it easier for you to check your mushrooms against the descriptions given with each species.

Every type of mushroom grows in the sort of soil that suits it and in the kind of location it likes best; in the sun or in the shade. But we cannot make hard and fast rules for such fickle subjects as these plants. One that you normally would expect to find in a wooded area will suddenly decide otherwise and start coming up in quantity in a nearby field; so habitat is not a good guide to what you can safely put in the pot.

A much safer guide is the season of the year when they come up, unless of course the weather is freakish. In a summer when the ground is baked dry, the normal flush of boleti and chanterelles cannot be expected. If the rain should come late, the summer mushrooms will not make their appearance at all, which is a great disappointment for enthusiasts, but at least it eliminates the confusion that would result if they came up at the same time as the species we find in the fall.

So from early spring until winter, in woods, forests, or fields, we can follow the progress of these strange creatures that are full of undiscovered possibilities.*

*Antibiotics are obtained from certain microscopic fungi, and there are others that may yet make an important contribution to world food supplies.

12

THE BEST WAY
TO USE MUSHROOMS

Mushrooms are much in demand as food and you rarely come across someone who does not appreciate the delicious concoctions made from them. However there are a few people who find them difficult to digest so they must not eat them too often nor be tempted to take too large a helping because in this, as in many other things, moderation is a virtue.

The food value of mushrooms is considerable. People with hearty appetites will have to be content with the recipes we give after each description, but, before trying them, here are a few general rules for getting the most out of what you collect.

The first thing to do is to sort the mushrooms according to what use will be made of them, either to be eaten at once or to be preserved. If you want to preserve some, choose only those young specimens that are firm and undamaged. The ones that are a little more advanced and do not look quite as good are the ones to eat right away.

From the ones you intend to eat at once you should pick out any that can be eaten raw. There are very few kinds because most mushrooms are indigestible, or even slightly poisonous, before they are cooked. There are one or two kinds that should be blanched in boiling water before further cooking, and some need to be dried for a short spell first.

When there is a big crop you can prepare mushrooms in various, different ways and eat them at the same meal, if you have enough patience to cook them. If not, then you can eat them at different meals in succession.

If firm-fleshed specimens are mixed up with the more fragile ones that need less cooking time, the latter will go mushy before the others are cooked. There are kinds with a strong flavor that blend well with additional seasonings like garlic, olive oil, and aromatic herbs. The more delicate ones are set off best with a little bit of butter.

Some types of mushrooms can be preserved easily using the old-fashioned, country methods that were the only ones available years ago. Others need all the resources of a modern kitchen.

Boleti, morels, helvellas, the Horn of Plenty, and the Fairy Ring Mushroom are easily dried if the temperature is right. Do not wash them but clean them with a knife. Split them in two or, in the case of boleti, cut them in thin slices. Put them in the sun on a tray, or string them on cotton thread so as not to be touching each other, and hang them up to dry. If the evenings are damp, bring them in before the dew settles on the grass. Continue the operation until the mushrooms are quite dry; that is, brittle. Put them in cans or sealed jars away from the light.

When you decide to use them it is best to soak them for 15 minutes in warm, salty water and after that cook them as though they were fresh.

Preserving by freezing

If you have a freezer, it is good for keeping chanterelles. Clean them and remove any earthy bits, put them in a plastic bag, squeeze out the air, and seal. Do not thaw when the time comes to cook them. You can also freeze other kinds, but it is advisable to cook them first.

Preserving by canning

Start by cooking the mushrooms using the recommended recipes, but stop before the cooking is completed and put them into glass canning jars and seal the lids in accordance with the manufacturer's instructions. Inside the jars, the mushrooms will give up additional liquid as they are processed. Put the jars in a pressure cooker for an hour and a half after the regulator valve indicates maximum temperature. Alternatively put the jars in a hot water bath for two and a half hours at 100° (212°F). This method is good for all kinds of mushrooms.

Preserving in vinegar

This is a suitable method for the chanterelle, the Delicious Milky Cap, and the Cup-Bearing Clavaria.

Blanch by plunging them for three minutes into boiling salted water. Rinse in cold water and let drain a few hours before packing them into a glass or earthenware jar. Meanwhile prepare some wine or malt vinegar by boiling it for five minutes with a bunch of parsley, a sprig of tarragon, a clove of garlic, and a few peppercorns. Allow the seasoned vinegar mixture to cool before pouring it over the mushrooms and covering the jar. This pickle goes well with cold meats.

In some countries mushrooms are preserved in salt or in oil but it is not common here.

IS THERE ANY DANGER
OF BEING POISONED?

By carefully reading the description of each species in this book and **meticulously observing the features that will ensure against error,** even a novice can gather and eat fungi with complete peace of mind.

Some rash collectors neglect these precautions and they make mistakes, so you ought to know what to do if it becomes necessary for you to act.

First you must find out if it really is a case of poisoning; some highly strung persons do in fact feel ill at the very thought of eating fungi, even though they are perfectly wholesome. Others may think they have been poisoned when it is simply a case of having eaten too much. Mushrooms are rich food. Quite harmless food like shrimp or lobster may cause trouble when eaten to excess.

In every case where a meal of fungi is followed by disorders that go beyond the consequences of eating too much, a doctor should be called at once. Swift action may well prevent many a mishap.

Symptoms may take the form of excitement similar to that of drunkenness, even though no alcohol has been consumed; abnormal secretions (tears or abundant perspiration); frequent vomiting and diarrhea accompanied by sharp pain; an intense thirst. These effects which may appear soon after eating mushrooms, are not really serious, unless the victim has been weakened by a previous illness.

If, however, several hours after the meal, sometimes the day following, your table companion finds his or her skin turning yellow and suffers from fainting fits or periods of sleep interrupted by convulsions, the outlook is serious and you must call the doctor with the utmost urgency. So, too, if the sick person has stomach pains, cold sweating, and giddiness.

We feel it necessary to describe this list of disorders which indicate mushroom poisoning so that everybody can help a possible victim. However the enthusiast must not be scared by this unhappy picture. **Accidents only happen when there has been lack of attention or prudence.** Since it is easy to avoid such accidents, we should put aside once and for all those unfortunate prejudices which these plants suffer from.

LIST OF SYMBOLS
FOR MAKING A QUICK CHECK

At the top left-hand corner of each descriptive sheet there is a small outline drawing of a mushroom showing the obvious features that will help the reader to find the description that fits a specimen.

Here is a list of these symbols and what they stand for:

Mushroom with gills, having a cap and a stem. The stem has neither volva nor ring.

Mushroom with gills, having a cap and a stem. The stem has a ring, but no volva at its base.

Mushroom with gills, having a cap and a stem. The stem has a volva at its base, but no ring.

Mushroom with gills, having a cap and a stem. The stem has both a ring, and a volva at its base.

Mushroom having a cap and a stem. The underside of the cap is covered with spines.

Mushroom having a cap and a stem. The underside of the cap is covered with tubes.

Ball-shaped mushroom.

Coral-shaped mushroom.

Sponge-shaped mushroom.

Cup-shaped mushroom.

ILLUSTRATED GLOSSARY

Adherent   Used to describe gills that have their vertical edge fixed to the stem.

Adnate   Synonym for *adherent.*

Cap   The top part of many kinds of fungi. It is often the edible part.

Cortina   The transparent veil that envelopes young specimens of certain species, thus giving them the name *Cortinarius.* The veil breaks as the fungus grows bigger, after which only traces of the veil remain on the stem and sometimes on the edge of the cap.

Decurrent   Used to describe gills that run down the stem for some distance without changing direction.

Emarginate   Applied to gills that have a decurrent tooth, more or less pronounced, just after their point of attachment to the stem.

Flakes   Synonym for *gills.*

Free   Used to describe gills attached to the cap but that do not touch the stem.

Gills   Flat-surfaced organs suspended vertically from the cap and that are arranged around the stem like the spokes of a wheel. The gills carry the spores, which are elements of reproduction for mushrooms.

equal, distant   equal, crowded   unequal   forked

Margin   The edge of the cap.

Milk	The liquid that comes out of some species when they are broken. It may be white or colored, sweet or bitter.
Pores	The visible extremities of the tubes, the ends of which give the underside of the cap its color.
Ring	A membrane surrounding the stem of some fungi (the Parasol and most Amanitas).
Spines	Very small organs (fractions of an inch) found on the underside of the cap in some species.
Spores	White or colored dust that is the element of reproduction in mushrooms. Where there are gills the spores are attached to them.
Squamous	Covered with scales.
Stem	The pillar-shaped part of a mushroom that supports the cap and that may be swollen to some extent.
Tubes	Fine tubes underneath the cap of some species (boleti). When the mushroom is developed they form a kind of moss that is quite firm. The tubes contain spores.
Umbonate	Refers to a cap with a slight pimple in the middle.
Volva	A fleshy bag found at the base of the stem in some species (most of the Amanitas).

THE SUBALPINUS

Hygrophorus marzuolus

Mushroom collecting starts early in the year for some people living in the mountains. Immediately at the beginning of spring when the snow melts, this handsome species begins to appear in pinewoods. Its early appearance is a great joy to mushroom hunters who have not been able to practice their sport since the end of the previous season.

Cap	Very light gray, almost white when young, becoming darker. Convex at first with involuted margin, then irregularly wavy. 2 to 4 inches across. Flesh thick and soft, marbled with gray.
Gills	Sparse, unequal, slightly decurrent, thick, white turning to gray.
Spores	White.
Stem	Stocky, somewhat conical, whitish turning to brownish-gray. Neither volva nor ring.
Habitat	Pinewoods in the mountains. In clusters.
Season	End of winter. Spring.
Special Features	Its early appearance. On account of this it cannot be confused with any other species.
Recipes	The Subalpinus is especially appreciated because it grows in northern and mountainous districts; even more so because it comes at a time when not only mushrooms but other vegetables are scarce. Its appearance is thus a real godsend in more ways than one. If you find enough of them you can eat them alone, lightly fried in butter. Otherwise a few can be added to meat or poultry, but first sauté them in a pan with cubes of bacon fat and small onions, then put them to simmer in the meat or poultry gravy to enhance the sauce.

*Often some moss or a leaf sticks
to the cap and keeps it
shaded, leaving an area without color
(see the picture at top right).*

MORELS AND GYROMITRAS

Morchella esculenta   *Gyromitra esculenta*

Morchella conica

If early spring has been sunny and the air is mild, you can expect to see strange little sponges on the fringes of woods or in the middle of dirt roads where patches of grass are growing. These are the much-prized, very delicate morels, thought by many connoisseurs to be the finest-tasting mushrooms one can eat.

Whether the cap be oval, practically touching the ground as in the round morel *(M. esculenta),* or whether it has a conical head on a slender stalk like the cone-shaped morel *(M. conica),* this mushroom is easily recognized by the fairly deep cavities between the riblike folds. Morels are hollow.

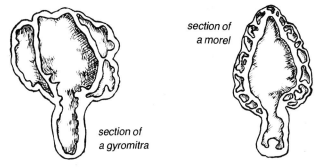

*section of
a morel*

*section of
a gyromitra*

They can only be confused with *Gyromitras,* a neighboring genus which for many years were sold under the name of morels. The *Gyromitra esculenta,* commonly called the False Morel or Brain Mushroom, is also good to eat, has a round head, is brown in color, and is rather bloated with wavy folds. The stem is whitish and irregular.

Special Features	Morels and gyromitras must not be eaten fresh. Let them dry for a few days and then soak them for five minutes in warm water just before cooking. You should also not eat gyromitras more than once a week. When dried, these mushrooms can be stored for months.
Recipes	Begin by sautéing them lightly in a little butter with no other seasoning than salt. If they are then mixed with a beaten egg you can transform a simple omelet into a dish of remarkable subtlety. They are also used to make a cream sauce that is an essential part of a chicken dish cooked with yellow wine* and morels, much beloved in the Jura mountains of France.

*a special local wine

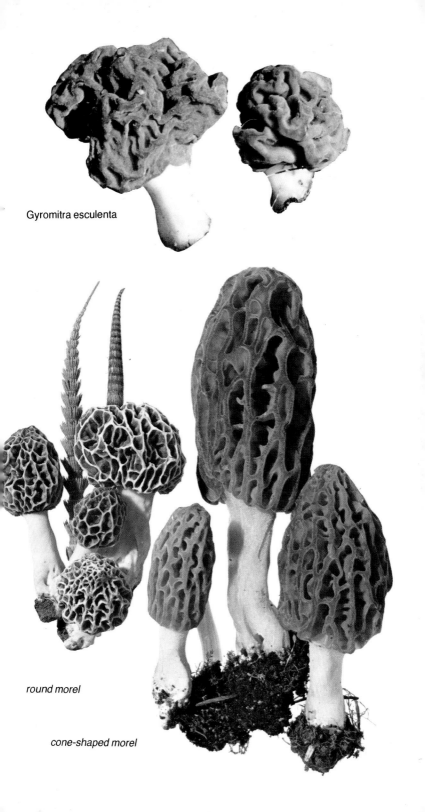

Gyromitra esculenta

round morel

cone-shaped morel

ST. GEORGE'S MUSHROOM

Lyophyllum (Tricholoma) Georgii

It is not a fact that this mushroom comes up only on the 23rd of April, but it is to be found only in the spring, although one may come across a few specimens in summer and, rarely, the occasional odd one in the fall. This species is temperamental; sometimes it comes up pure white and sometimes it is shaded with rust or lilac-colored patches. The color is deeper toward the center.

Cap	Pure white, creamy white, buff, sometimes stained brown or mauve-gray. Thick, convex becoming flattened. Margin incurved when young. Smells of fresh flour. 2 to 5 inches across.
Gills	White, crowded, often forked, emarginate.
Spores	White.
Stem	White or whitish, short, thick, cylindrical, slightly swollen at the base, fleshy. Neither volva nor ring.
Habitat Season	Fields, forests, or clearings. Grows in circles. Spring, rarely in summer.
Special Features	Can be confused with the poisonous Patouillard's Inocybe (*Inocybe Patouillardi*), which appears at the same time. The table below indicates the differences:

Note	ST. GEORGE'S MUSHROOM	PATOUILLARD'S INOCYBE
Spores	White.	Reddish-brown.

Recipes	The flesh, although delicate in taste, is somewhat indigestible. Blanch this mushroom in boiling water before proceeding further. After cooking in butter it can be mixed with eggs in an omelet, or it may be served up with a meat dish.

Fungi cannot be sold freely in France. Local laws in each town determine which species may be sold. There are regions where certain kinds grow in abundance and they are offered for sale to the housewife, but these same mushrooms, just as wholesome, are not allowed to be marketed in other districts. Before being put on the market all mushrooms are submitted to a quality controller who examines them one by one.

You have a good chance of finding the St. George's Mushroom in the same fairy rings where there were Bluelegs (page 80) the previous fall.

THE FAIRY RING MUSHROOM

Marasmius oreades

If this is sometimes called the "false Mousseron" it does not mean that you must be suspicious of it as of a false friend. It is meant to distinguish it from the true St. George's Mushroom (see page 24), also edible, but found almost only in the spring. It has a small, buff-colored cap on top of a long slender stalk and it attracts attention by growing in colonies forming circles or rings in the middle of the fields. You can often gather a sizeable crop in quite a small area.

Cap	Conical then flattened, sometimes umbonate. Fawn-colored when wet, it becomes light buff when the air is dry. The margin is slightly striated and the center may be a little darker. 1 to 2½ inches across.
Gills	Free, sparse, unequal, cream becoming fawn.
Spores	White.
Stem	Slender, elegant, fibrous, firm, the base often downy. Neither volva nor ring.
Habitat	Usually grows in rings even though only part of the circumference may be seen. Pastures, roadsides.
Season	From spring to fall.
Special Features	Its characteristic of growing in circles in fields. The sparse and widely separated gills, as well as its buff or fawn color, prevent confusion with other species.
Recipes	Throw out the stem, which is woody. The cap has a most agreeable taste and an omelet made from these little mushrooms is a delight. Brown them lightly in butter first. Add them to the gravy of roast poultry, or put them in a stew to add a woody aroma that also improves the taste. Dried and ground to a powder they can be used as a condiment in stews.

The names *Hag Tracks* or *Fairy Rings* given to circles of mushrooms like these show that in former times a popular belief attributed supernatural qualities to fungi. In fact, the underground part of these plants spreads out like the spokes of a wheel and the mushrooms themselves appear at the circumference. This is why the circle grows bigger each year.

THE RUSSULAS

There are many varieties to be found in a wide range of colors—brown, yellow, red, slate-gray, or purple. Occasionally several different shades are blended together in one specimen. As soon as you can recognize the species, all you need do is to taste a small piece of one. You can tell at once if it is sweet or bitter or peppery.

We recommend two different kinds:

THE BLUE AND YELLOW RUSSULA

Russula cyanoxantha

Cap	Color varies from deep purple to dark green and slate gray, often in the same specimen. Dome-shaped then cup-shaped becoming flattened. Slightly slimy in wet weather. 2 to 6 inches across.
Gills	White, adnate, thick, sometimes forked.
Spores	White.
Stem	Cylindrical, white, firm becoming hollow. Neither volva nor ring.
Habitat	Woods.
Season	Summer, fall.
Special Features	The sweet taste, which distinguishes it from similar Russulas.
Recipes	R. cyanoxantha can be grilled over glowing embers. Cut off the stem, turn the cap on its back, and sprinkle the gills with a few drops of oil and a pinch of salt. They can also be sauted in a pan with oil or lard mixed with finely chopped shallots.

Russulas can soon be
recognized from their
general appearance
in spite of
different coloring

29

THE GREENISH RUSSULA

Russula virescens

Cap	Domed, becoming flat and curved inward toward the center. Cream-colored flecked with light green. 2 to 6 inches across.
Gills	Free, white, equal, occasionally forked.
Spores	White.
Stem	Cylindrical, white, firm becoming spongy.
Habitat	Woods, clearings.
Season	Summer.
Special Features	Cannot be confused with *Amanita phalloides* if the following points are closely studied:

Note	RUSSULA VIRESCENS	AMANITA PHALLOIDES
Cap	Leek-green pattern; Crackled, matt.	Yellowish-green; smooth, silky.
Stem	Short and stocky. Neither volva nor ring.	Tall and slim. Volva and ring.

Russula virescens

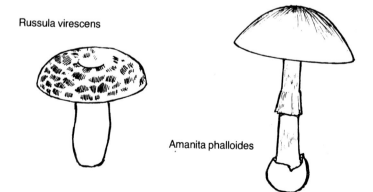

Amanita phalloides

Recipes   The same as for the *R. cyanoxantha* (see page 28).
Most people consider this to be the best of the Russulas and some think it rivals the best of mushrooms.
Since the flesh is firm it can be preserved easily either by canning or freezing.

In our time we can hardly imagine a world without bread or wine. History frequently mentions civilizations that, although they knew about fermented drinks, ate unleavened pancakes. It is said that when the Egyptians used flour that had been contaminated by the flood waters of the Nile they noticed that the bread swelled up. So it was that yeast, which is a microscopic fungus, for the first time became part of the baker's art. As for the fungi that produce alcoholic fermentation, we know that Noah already held it in high esteem. . . .

The innate faculty of fungi to destroy certain refuse may enable us in the future to solve the vexing problem of pollution due to the accumulation of refuse in our big cities. This is the direction in which researchers are looking at the moment.

THE CHANTERELLE

Cantherellus cibarius

In June they start coming up like yellow flowers half-hidden by moss, on banks, under birch trees, or more usually under foliage.

Cap	The shape varies with the individual, convex becoming umbonate and finally funnel-shaped with uneven margin. Color varies from yellowish-white to deep gold. This mushroom is all in one piece and is of the same color and consistency throughout. 2 to 4 inches across.
Gills	Decurrent, branching, thick, hardly showing on the cap and of the same color.
Spores	White.
Stem	Follows on from the cap without any sign of a break. Same color as the cap. Cylindrical or slightly conical tapering toward the base. Firm.
Habitat	Woods, banks, clearings.
Season	Summer.

Special Features	Can be confused with the False Chanterelle (*Clitocybe aurantica*) which, although it is not poisonous, is not edible or with the Olive Tree Clitocybe (*Clitocybe illudens*), which, on the contrary, can cause trouble. Here are the differences:	

Note	CHANTHERELLUS CIBARIUS	OLIVE TREE CLITOCYBE
Habitat	On the ground all over the country.	At the foot of, and on tree stumps (not only of olive trees).
The way it grows	Alone, or grouped with a few others.	**In tufts.**
Gills	Branching folds, not very pronounced.	Unequal and crowded.
Season	Summer.	Summer, fall, and winter.

There is a different variety, the Yellow-Stemmed Chanterelle (*Cantherellus tubaeformis*), which looks like a small brown funnel on top of a brownish stem. It can only be confused with the Horn of Plenty, which is also edible (see page 72).

Recipes	As a rule, chanterelles are full of water, which should be eliminated by putting them in a pan without any fat and letting them cook until the liquid has evaporated. Sautéd in butter, they go well in an omelet. Cooked in lard with finely chopped shallots, they go well with poultry or pork chops.

THE BOLETI

These are some of the most sought after and most frequently picked of all mushrooms. Amateurs are keen on them but they are also imported in large quantities from Europe. Boleti are easily recognized by the tubes that cover the underside of the cap. You can see the ends of these tubes (the pores), which form a colored surface.

Contrary to popular belief there are no poisonous boleti and, although in some species the flesh turns blue, that does not in the least affect their eating quality. There are two kinds of boleti to be avoided:

1. The Devil's Boletus (*Boletus satanas*), which is indigestible and can cause a stomach ache.

2. The bitter boleti or peppery ones (*Boletus piperatus*) because they are quite inedible and completely spoil the taste of any dish to which they may be added. As in the case of the Russulas, you need only put a tiny piece of a boletus on the tip of your tongue to know what the taste is like. Fortunately there are not many kinds of boleti with a bad taste, and, what is more, all the bitter ones have pink spores.

THE STEINPILZ, KING BOLETUS, OR CEP

Boletus edulis

Since this mushroom is so common in the Bordeaux region of France, it is often called the "Bordeaux Cep," but fortunately it grows in other parts of the world too. It is usually considered to be the best of the boleti, although a few neighboring species are also thought of very highly. The *Boletus edulis* is a handsome mushroom with a buff-colored cap, but it can also be dark brown, in which case it is called the Bronzed Boletus (*Boletus aereus*).

Cap	Rounded, then a spreading dome, buff or dark brown, matt downy. 3 to 8 inches across or even bigger.
Pores	Whitish, then pale yellow turning greenish with age.
Flesh	White. Does not turn blue when cut.
Habitat	Woods, clearings, roadsides.
Season	A flush in June and another one during the summer. Fall.

Bronzed Boletus

King Boletus

THE SLIPPERY JACK

Boletus luteus   Boletus granulatus

Because it grows in groups, there is a chance of gathering a good crop of Slippery Jacks when the more reputed kinds of mushrooms are not to be found. There are two closely related species: *B. luteus* and *B. granulatus.* The first has a peculiar and exceptional feature for a boletus; it has a veil that hides the tubes in a young specimen. This membrane tears and falls as a sort of ring around the stem as the mushroom grows bigger and this gives it the pretty nickname of "The Veiled Nun" (see photo opposite).

In wet weather this mushroom becomes water-logged and soggy, but this does nothing to alter the taste. As in the case of all boleti, it is better to remove the tubes if the cap is fully open.

Cap	Light reddish-brown, domed then flat, covered with a slimy skin that can easily be removed. 2 to 4 inches across.
Stem	Cylindrical, whitish or pale yellow, covered with small granules, deeper in color toward the top or between the ring and the cap. The ring clings to the stem but leaves little trace.
Pores	Pale yellow.
Flesh	Soft, pale yellow, does not turn blue, slightly acid taste.
Habitat	In long grass and near pine trees. Often in groups.
Season	Summer, fall.
Recipes	Remove the slimy skin from the cap. The flesh, which is somewhat soft but tastes good, can be cooked in the same way as the King Boletus (see page 40)

THE RED-CRACKED BOLETUS

Boletus chrysenteron

Not as large as the King Boletus and less sought after, this mushroom is nevertheless welcome in a poor season when it is difficult to find much else.

Cap	Brown, downy or cracked. When cracked, the yellow flesh tinged with red shows through the darker patches. Up to 3½ inches across.
Pores	Wide at the ends compared to the imperceptible tips of a young King Boletus (see page 34).
Stem	Rather weak, yellow stained pink or red at the base.
Flesh	Yellowish turning blue when cut, red beneath the cap.
Habitat	Woods.
Season	Summer, fall.
Recipes	See page 40.

THE ROUGH-STEMMED BOLETUS

Boletus scaber

Softer than the other boletes, this one is the least sought after and for that reason it is only worth gathering if the better kinds are not to be had.

Cap	Fawn, buff, brown, or orange. Conical then domed 2 to 4 inches across.
Pores	Whitish then turning gray with black spots.
Stem	Tall and slim, slightly swollen at the base, covered with darker scales standing out from a white background.
Flesh	Soft, turning mauve-gray then black when cut.
Habitat	Gloomy, damp woods. Banks.
Season	Summer, fall.
Recipes	Throw out the tough stem. Pick only young specimens; they taste best. The flesh turns black when cooked. You may be put off by the color, but it makes no difference to the flavor (see page 40).

THE RED-STEMMED BOLETUS
Boletus erythropus

The flesh of this boletus turns blue and then green when cut and anybody who is scared by the color change need not be. It is easy to distinguish this mushroom from the indigestible Devil's Boletus (*Boletus satanas*). Its eating qualities are not to be despised and anyway the original color comes back when it is cooked.

Cap	Domed, then a flattened cupola, **dark brown,** and downy. (The cap of the Devil's Boletus is **grayish-white**) 4 to 6 inches across.
Pores	Dark red turning olive green with age.
Stem	Thick and clublike, yellow and orange, flecked with red; a neighboring variety has a stem with a thin red lattice.
Flesh	Yellow turning blue then green when cut. Turns back to yellow when cooked or when dried for storing.
Habitat	Open woods, roadsides.
Season	Summer, fall.

Recipes for all kinds of boleti: The youngest specimens have the firmest flesh so if the tubes have started to go soft it is better to remove them. The King Boletus is just as tasty however way you cook it—cut them into thin slices then sauté in butter or olive oil, either alone or with finely chopped garlic and parsley. The varieties that are not so good are improved by being more highly seasoned. Boleti improve all meat and poultry dishes whether they are used to season the gravy or whether served as a separate vegetable. An omelet of boleti is delicious.

Stuffed Boleti: Finely chop the stems and mix them with the butter used for snails; that is, butter with finely ground garlic and parsley worked into it. Turn the caps on their backs and stuff them with this mixture, then cover with a good layer of breadcrumbs and bake in an earthenware dish in a moderate oven. Twenty to thirty minutes of cooking will be long enough depending upon the size of the mushrooms.

Boleti Fritters: Cut the stems in rounds of or just less than half an inch thick and the caps into slices of the same thickness. Put in an earthenware dish and moisten with a marinade made as follows: two tablespoons of olive oil, the juice of half a lemon, salt, pepper, and chopped parsley. After an hour take out the mushroom pieces and dip them in a fritter batter. Deep fry.

This mushroom is delicious to eat.
Do not confuse it with the Devil's Boletus described below.

Here is a description of the Devil's Boletus that will help you avoid this not very desirable mushroom:

Cap	Domed, then a spreading cupola, **grayish-white** 4 to 8 inches across, sometimes even larger.
Pores	Yellow in very young specimens but **soon bright red.**
Stem	Short, clublike, swollen at the base, yellow at the ends and red in the middle, the upper part is covered with a red network.
Flesh	Creamy-white, turns blue when cut.
Habitat & Season	Deciduous woods. Summer, fall.

THE ORANGE-BROWN LACTARIUS

Lactarius volemus

Large quantities of white milk flow from this mushroom when it is broken open. The French call it "Little cow." This milk is a peculiarity it shares with other Lactarius mushrooms we shall meet later on. Beginners will find it a godsend because none of the mushrooms with milk are poisonous, although some of them are too bitter to be eaten. How can the good-tasting ones be recognized? It is the simplest thing in the world: put a tiny piece on the tip of your tongue and you will soon find out! If all goes well you can go ahead and pick without fear.

Cap	Red and downy, darker toward the center. Convex becoming funnel-shaped. Average 1½ to 4 inches across. The flesh turns brown when cut.
Gills	Adnate, unequal, crowded, cream with brown patches.
Spores	White.
Stem	Cylindrical, cream near the gills red lower down, firm. Neither volva nor ring.
Habitat	Woods.
Season	Summer.
Special Features	Gives a sweet-smelling, white milk when broken.
Recipes	May be eaten raw. Can be included in salads or served with fresh cream flavored with a teaspoon of lemon juice. Lightly browned in oil with chopped shallots it goes well with roast pork. Pickled in vinegar you can eat it in the same way as gherkins.
	A country recipe for the Delicious Milky Cap (see page 57) is also good for this one. Grill them with the caps bottom side up over hot charcoal, or better still over the glowing embers of vine prunings.* Sprinkle a few drops of olive oil, salt, and pepper on the gills, and do not forget a speck of garlic.

*In wine-growing regions it is quite common to burn the prunings of the vineyards.

Mushrooms were probably known to man from the very beginning of time. There is documentary evidence, however, only as far back as the fifth century B.C. The celebrated Greek physician Hippocrates tells us that in his time mushrooms were used as medicine. The Roman poets Martial and Juvenal were fond of eating and they very much appreciated the taste of mushrooms. Later on, in the first century A.D., a Greek doctor wrote an important book on the use of mushrooms in medicine. He pointed out that even the best of them may prove to be difficult to digest if they are not eaten in moderation. For good measure he gives a decidedly original recipe for greedy people who have eaten too much of this delicious food, and here it is: make a mixture of honey and dried poultry droppings ground to a powder, then moisten the mix with a few drops of vinegar. We suppose that anyone swallowing this mixture would quickly be relieved of his pains . . . . and of his mushrooms too!

THE MEADOW MUSHROOM

Psalliota (Agaricus) campestris

These are the ancestors of the cultivated mushroom and they have more taste than their more civilized offspring. The species comes in several varieties that differ in their firmness and in the color of the cap, which can be either lighter or darker and its surface either smooth or scaly.

Cap	White, cream, sometimes with brown patches, darker toward the center, silky. Spherical at first, then domed and finally flat. No bigger than a pea when it comes out of the ground, it can grow to 3 or 4 inches in diameter. The flesh turns pink when cut.
Gills	Salmon pink, almost white, turning to grayish-mauve and to purplish-brown with age. Crowded, free, fragile.
Spores	Dark purplish-brown.
Stem	White, cylindrical, solid. The ring is cottony and rubs off easily, pieces of it adhere to the stem and to the edge of the cap when the mushroom is not fully open. No volva.
Habitat	Pastures grazed by animals, any place that has been manured.
Season	Summer, fall.
Special Features	Unfortunately, it is in gathering Meadow Mushrooms that careless people find the most dangerous of all fungi, and it is important to recognize *Amanita phalloides* in order to avoid it (see page 86). However, you do not need to be very observant to see the difference between these two species, which are not really alike:

Note	MEADOW MUSHROOM	AMANITA PHALLOIDES
Color	Pinkish or yellowish-white.	Greenish-white or light green (sometimes white) to olive green.
Stem	Ring cottony or absent. No volva.	Skirt-shaped ring. **Volva.**
Gills	Mauve to purple.	**White, uneven.**
Spores	Dark purplish-brown.	**White.**

*When the mushroom is old (photograph top
right), the gills turn black. It is better
not to eat them when they are like this.*

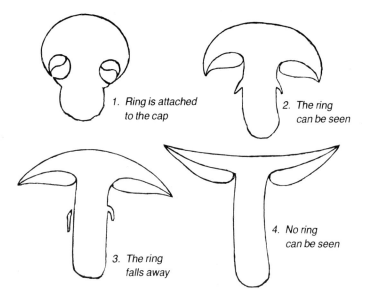

1. Ring is attached to the cap

2. The ring can be seen

3. The ring falls away

4. No ring can be seen

Section of a Meadow Mushroom showing four stages in its development.

Recipes

They can be sautéd simply in butter, but they also go well with meat in gravy, rabbit, and poultry. In this case cut them into four and brown with cubes of bacon fat and small onions before putting them to cook with the rest.

Velouté (soup): Chop up the raw mushrooms. Brown them lightly in butter, add salt and 6 ounces of boiling water per person and per tablespoon of chopped mushroom. Cook for five minutes then pass through a sieve, squashing the mushrooms to make the juice come out. Stir in half a glass of fresh cream and bind with the yolk of one egg. Crôutons (little cubes of fried bread) add to the attraction of this dish, which is even better if you can use chicken broth in place of water.

As an exception to the rule that almost all mushrooms must be properly cooked, the Meadow Mushroom can be eaten raw. Cut caps and stems into thin slices and place in a salad bowl with salt, pepper, the juice of half a lemon, and two tablespoons of fresh cream and a few sprigs of chopped chervil. A finely sliced apple adds a pleasant note to this succulent salad.

Meadow Mushrooms are also delicious sautéd in butter and with the pan deglazed with cognac and cream. It is an elegant accompaniment to a roast beef or chicken.

THE HORSE MUSHROOM

Psalliota (Agaricus) arvensis

There is a particularly sturdy variety of the Meadow Mushroom known as the Horse Mushroom or Plowed Land Mushroom. The cap can be as much as eight inches across.

Recipes   Horse Mushrooms can be grilled over hot charcoal. Cut off the stem and turn the cap gills side up. Add a small amount of olive oil or a teaspoon of melted butter and a pinch of salt and pepper.

THE CAESARS' MUSHROOM
or ROYAL MUSHROOM

Amanita caesarea

Although rarely found in northern areas, this is not to be missed if you have a chance. When it first pushes through the soil it looks like an egg, which then breaks open to reveal the most famous of all mushrooms.

Cap	Orange-colored, domed at first then a regular cupola and finally flattening. Striated margin. 4 to 6 inches across.
Gills	Sulphur yellow, free, unequal.
Spores	White.
Stem	Yellow, yellow ring, white volva.
Habitat	Woods, clearings.
Season	Summer, fall.
Special Features	A few well-defined features prevent it from being mistaken for another mushroom, the Fly Amanita *(Amanita muscaria)*, which is poisonous:

Note	CAESARS' MUSHROOM	FLY AMANITA
Cap	Orange-colored, smooth or with a fragment of volva.	Bright red with white spots.
Gills	Yellow.	White.
Stem Ring	Yellow.	White.

Recipes	The flavor of this mushroom is so delicate that it would be a great pity to mask it by complicated cookery. Simply browned in butter and salted it is a truly remarkable dish.

It is called the Caesars' Mushroom because
Roman emperors were so fond of it.

BLUSHED RED AMANITA

Amanita rubescens

Nearly as delicious as the Caesar's Mushroom and a good consolation prize if you fail to find them.

Cap	Ovoid, flecked with white spots that almost cover it, then domed. More or less wine-colored. Flesh white, reddening where bruised. 3 to 6 inches across.
Gills	White, crowded, equal, with red patches.
Spores	White.
Stem	The swollen base is pointed at the bottom. Often attacked by insects and stained reddish-brown. Skirt-shaped ring. No volva.
Habitat	Woods, clearings, forests.
Season	Summer, fall.
Special Features	Can only be confused with the False Blusher *(Amanita pantherina)*, which is deadly poisonous:

Note	BLUSHED RED AMANITA	FALSE BLUSHER
Stem	With a cone, no volva.	Volva with folds.
Flesh	**Turns red.**	**White.**

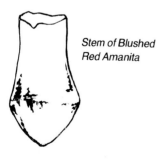

Stem of Blushed Red Amanita

Stem of False Blusher

Recipes   Splendid eating. Browned in a frying pan with butter and salt, it can be counted among the best.

THE SHEATHED AMANITA
or GRISSETTE

Amanita vaginata

These mushrooms are so fragile that they must be picked with care. They tend to be squashed by heavier specimens and they should be kept apart from them and the earth on their stems.

Cap	It comes out of the ground looking like a big bullet and opens out into a cupola. The color is light gray (as its name implies) but there is also a buff-colored version just as common and just as good to eat. The margin of the cap is striated and the cap may retain a scrap of the volva.
Gills	White, free.
Spores	White.
Stem	Slender, fragile, white or grayish, fibrous, hollow; thin where it joins the cap. Very long volva, no ring.
Habitat	Fields, edges of woods, clearings.
Season	Summer, fall.

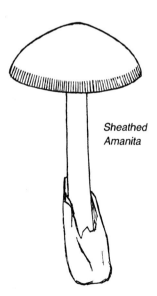

Sheathed
Amanita

False
Blusher

Special
Features

The Sheathed Amanita could be confused with the False Blusher, which is deadly poisonous (see drawing on opposite page), but there are differences:

Note	SHEATHED AMANITA	FALSE BLUSHER
Cap	Buff or gray.	Brownish covered with white spots.
Stem	Long volva. No ring.	Rounded volva with folds on top. A ring.

Recipes

This mushroom has a delicate flavor that is retained if it is lightly cooked in butter. One of the best.

55

THE DELICIOUS MILKY CAP
or SAFFRON MILK CAP

Lactarius deliciosus

Appearances are not always helpful. Tucked away in rough grass at the foot of pine trees, this mushroom looks like a small, orange-colored disc stained with verdigris. When the flesh is broken, a bright orange milk, which soon turns green, oozes out. Do not be put off by this alarming appearance, which hides a good, honest mushroom. One variety of this species—the Red-Juice Milky Cap *(Lactarius sanguifluus)*—has milk that is decidedly red, nevertheless some people prefer it.

Cap	Fleshy, domed, with incurved margin, later becoming cup-shaped. Orange-colored with darker concentric circles. Turns verdigris at the least touch or bruise. Goes green with age. The flesh is firm. 2 to 6 inches across.
Gills	Decurrent, crowded, orange-colored with green stains.
Spores	White.
Stem	Cylindrical, orange-colored, fairly tough, becoming bulbous. Neither volva nor ring.
Habitat	Pinewoods.
Season	Summer, fall.
Special Features	Like all the Lactarii, it can be distinguished from the ones similar to it but which have a bitter milk by tasting a small piece.

Lactarius deliciosus

Lactarius sanguifluus

Recipes   When cut into slices and sautéd with cubes of bacon fat and small onions, this firm-fleshed mushroom makes a pleasant garnish for meat dishes. Often it is grilled over a fire after cutting off the stem, a small amount of olive oil poured on the gills, plus salt and pepper—a favorite recipe in some areas.

THE COMMON LACCARIA
or WAXY LACCARIA
Laccari laccata

The bright purple or salmon pink of these little mushrooms adds a cheerful note to the undergrowth. Since they usually come up in large quantity, their numbers make up for their small size.

Cap	Purple, or salmon pink, rounded and slightly flattened like a small, round button. The margin curves in at first then opens out in waves, becoming flat. A small hollow in the center.
Gills	Same color as the cap. Broad, sparse, unequal, adnate.
Spores	White.
Stem	Same color as the cap. Long, thin, fibrous then hollow. Neither volva nor ring.
Habitat	Woods.
Season	Summer, fall.
Special Features	Although it is much more slender, it could be mistaken, on account of its color, for a Wood Blewit (see page 82) or a Violet Cortinarius (not described), both of which are edible.
Recipes	Throw out the fibrous stem. The caps taste good cooked in butter and added to an omelet or put in a stew.

In France, mushroom hunting is a national pastime. In recent years hordes of mushroom gatherers have invaded the countryside during the season and there has been trouble between the local inhabitants and motorists coming from the towns especially for the picking. The mayors of some villages have established regulations to control mushroom picking. In the countryside in some areas on a Sunday it is estimated that as many as ten thousand people strip everything they can find in the woods. The result is a massive destruction of species that would continue to thrive for the benefit of all if picking could be controlled.

The amethyst variety

THE SHAGGY MANE

Coprinus comatus

They look like big white cigars covered with fawn-colored scales and here and there fluffy tufts of the same color. Shaggy Manes will push up on waste ground, under a hedge, or in some neglected corner of the garden. They stand up in regiments, stiff and straight, the young ones at the feet of their ancestors, as the old ones let the fringe of their blackened caps fall away in drops of ink.

Cap	Egg-shaped, upright. Never opens out. White or whitish with fawn-colored scales. Height 2 to 8 inches.
Gills	Free, white, pink turning to black.
Spores	Black.
Stem	Long, thicker at the base, white, whitish or pink. Fibrous. Ring thin and free, soon disappearing. No volva.
Habitat	Hedges, paths, roadsides, rubbish dumps.
Season	Summer, fall.
Special Features	When old, it liquifies into black ink. Because of this, only young specimens are good to eat. They must be used immediately after picking.
Recipes	On account of its fragility, this fungus is best cooked in butter with a little salt and nothing else. Alcohol must not be drunk when Shaggy Manes are eaten.

Although you should avoid eating any fungus you do not recognize for certain, it is recommended that you not senselessly destroy any species. Even poisonous fungi have a role to play in the balance of nature. They speed up the decomposition of refuse and enable trees and other plants to find nourishment in the soil enriched by their action. People who kick over mushrooms they do not like the look of may satisfy their own ill temper, but they certainly do not help the overall ecology of the area.

Top left, a fully developed specimen.
The gills have turned black and are turning to liquid.
It is no longer fit to eat.

BERKELEY'S CORTINARIUS

Cortinarius praestans

A cortina, as has been mentioned, is a temporary veil that joins the stem to the margin of the cap. This hides the gills in young specimens. Later the veil breaks, leaving only a very slight trace on the stem. It is sometimes very difficult to identify this species from the traces left by the veil, which are almost invisible. For this reason it is better to rely on other characteristics, especially the color of the spores.

Cap	Fleshy, convex, then flattened, slightly wrinkled and slimy when wet. Coppery-brown with a hint of purple. Striated margin.
Gills	Adnate, emarginate, unequal, lilac turning brownish.
Spores	Rust-colored.
Stem	White with pale lilac streaks, thick with bulbous base, joined to the cap by a cortina when young (hence its name). The veil tears when the mushroom expands and sometimes leaves no trace on the stem. No volva.
Habitat	Woods.
Season	Summer, fall.
Special Features	All the Cortinarii are edible except one, which is quite as dangerous as *Amanita phalloides* and for that reason we should get to know it: The Mountain or Golden Cortinarius *(Cortinarius orellanus)*:

Note	BERKELEY'S CORTINARIUS	GOLDEN CORTINARIUS
Gills	Numerous and crowded.	Sparse.
Stem	Swollen at the foot, pale lilac in color.	Cylindrical, yellow to golden, darker in the middle.

Recipes	Berkeley's Cortinarius is good cooked in oil with or without shallots and chopped parsley. If you put them in with the meat they should be sautéd in lard first.

THE SPREADING–HEDGEHOG MUSHROOM

Dentinum (Hydnum) repandum

When looking for chanterelles you might find that, without noticing, you had picked a Spreading-Hedgehog Mushroom. No harm would have been done since they are both edible and there are those who prefer the Spreading-Hedgehog Mushroom because the flesh is slightly firmer.

Cap	Light chamois in color, sometimes almost white, umbonate or flat, irregular. The underside of the cap is made of short, soft spines (about 1/16 inch in length) that come away easily when scratched with the fingernail.
Stem	Same color as the cap to which it is joined without any clear demarcation.
Habitat	Woods.
Season	Late summer, fall.
Special Features	The spines on the underside of the cap look like a sponge. There is no possibility of confusion with other mushrooms except with neighboring species having the same sort of spines, and they are not poisonous.
Recipes	Because of the firmness of the flesh, the mushroom needs cooking longer than the chanterelle, but otherwise they are both treated alike. They can be mixed together because the taste is similar; this is often useful when both sorts are scarce.

We all know that mushrooms, like other good things, should not be eaten to excess. However there are people in the world who seem to have adapted very well to their favorite food. It is said that years ago the lumberjacks of the Black Forest in Germany ate practically nothing else. Perhaps they did not have anything else to eat, but it does show that, willingly or not, their mode of living proved the nutritional value of mushrooms. Man is not alone in liking them. There are slugs that enjoy even the most poisonous species. A particular breed of ant goes as far as to cultivate fungi on rotting leaves.

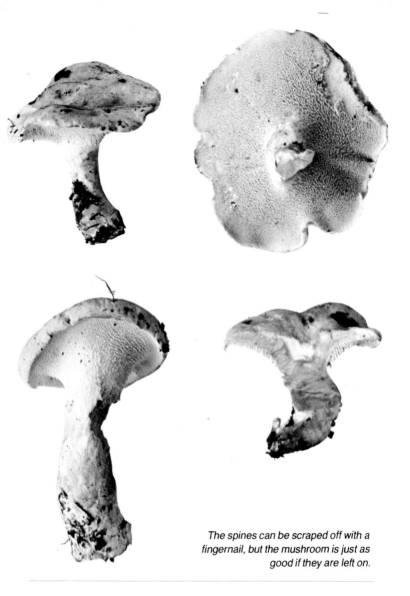

The spines can be scraped off with a fingernail, but the mushroom is just as good if they are left on.

Mushrooms are difficult subjects for cultivation, if we except the Meadow Mushroom, often called the Button Mushroom. Nevertheless some species have been harvested from specially prepared compost, but not with any regularity. Let us rejoice in the happy independence of the mushroom fraternity. What would happen to the great rush for the woods on a fine summer morning if you could grow chanterelles like green beans in your backyard garden?

THE GEM-STUDDED PUFFBALL

Lycoperdon perlatum

Puffballs look like small white pears planted pointed end down in dead leaves or moss, and they let out a dark brown powder when they are fully ripe. When the flesh is still white and firm, they can be eaten but they do not have much taste.

Recipes   Having but little taste they should be reinforced with herbs, condiments, and spices. Cut into slices and fried in oil, they are quickly improved by adding chopped garlic and parsley.

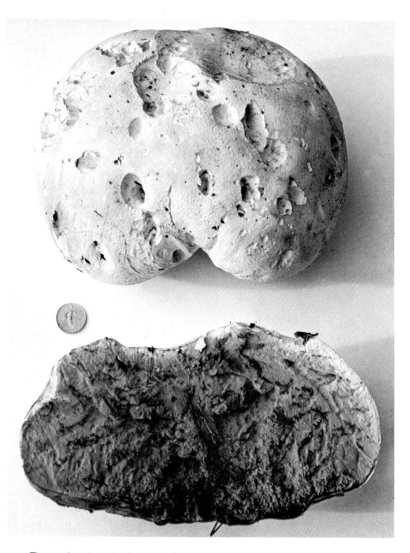

The section above is of a ripe puffball. It is not fit to eat in this condition.

THE GIANT PUFFBALL

Lycoperdon gigantea

Sometimes in a field one comes across a big white lump the size of a handball or even larger. This is the Giant Puffball. If the flesh is still firm there is enough to feed the whole family—even a big one! If it has gone too far, the best thing is to give it back to nature in the hope that some of the spores may find the right conditions to develop and so another year this fine mushroom will be the delight of whoever finds it.

THE HELVELLAS

Helvella crispa and others

Sometimes these are called Fall Morels even though their caps are not so deeply indented as the real morel. Actually their caps consist of a thin wafer twisted up in all directions to form an irregular mitre. The stem is deeply ridged, with thick ribs.

Two kinds are normally found, one is whitish—the Common Helvella *(Helvella crispa)*—and the other is dark gray or black—the Elfin Saddle *(Helvella lacunosa)*. Both are edible and come up in the fall on roadsides, in ditches, and under hedges.

Whatever the color—white, brown, gray, or black—the quality of Helvellas does not vary.

They may remind us of morels but they are not nearly as good. Cooked with a roast chicken, Helvellas are tasty. Otherwise brown them in butter and just before serving add a spoonful or two of fresh cream, depending on how many mushrooms there are. Cooked like this they can take the place of morels-in-cream for garnishing a chicken. They also make a good omelet.

THE MAN-ON-HORSEBACK

Tricholoma flavovirens (equestre)

This mushroom likes being near pine trees so that is the place to look, although it sometimes hides in long grass.

Cap	Pale yellow, convex then flattened, covered with small brown scales close together at the center. The flesh has no smell. 1½ to 4 inches across.
Gills	Yellow, crowded, emarginate, unequal.
Spores	White.
Stem	Yellow, stocky, firm. Neither volva nor ring.
Habitat	Pinewoods, sandy soil.
Season	Late summer, fall.
Special Features	The Sulphur Tricholoma *(Tricholoma sulfureum)*, which is inedible, is similar in appearance. There are features to distinguish between them:

Note	MAN-ON-HORSEBACK	SULPHUR TRICHOLOMA
Cap	Dotted with brown scales.	Smooth.
Gills	Numerous, crowded.	Sparse, thick.
Smell	No noticeable smell.	Strong smell of gas.

Recipes	Easily cooked with butter, oil, or bacon fat, with chopped shallots and parsley. Blends well with meat.
	If you like spicy dishes, try this one: Cut the mushrooms in slices and brown in a tablespoon of olive oil. Next pour in a glass of good, dry white wine and add lemon juice, a lump of sugar, a few coriander seeds, and a hint of Cayenne pepper. Served cold, this makes a good hors d'oeuvre.

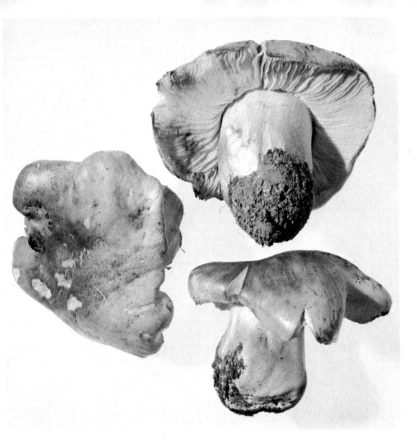

The same species of mushroom can grow taller and slimmer, depending on whether it is growing in long or short grass.

THE HORN OF PLENTY

Craterellus cornucopioides

Neither its appearance nor its nickname "Trumpet of Death" do justice to this excellent mushroom, which for good measure comes up in great masses when climatic conditions are right.

Cap	Like a trumpet or a bell-mouthed flute, irregular, black, gray, or dark brown. Splits along its length when pulled apart. ¾ to 3 inches across.
Gills	The outside surface of the cap replaces these. It is dark gray and covered with raised veins.
Spores	White, covering the outside of the mushroom. Put a specimen on a sheet of dark paper to collect them.
Stem	The tube on the end of the trumpet.
Habitat	Damp woods. Often in groups that spread over several square yards.
Season	Late summer, fall.
Special Features	Because of its peculiar shape it can only be mixed up with the gray species of chanterelles, which are also edible.
Recipes	A favorite in the kitchen, the Horn of Plenty, even though slightly tough, can be sautéd in butter or lard, served plain or garnished with chopped shallots or garlic and parsley. Put in an omelet they deepen the color but add incomparable flavor. In a restaurant, when truffles are often too expensive or are unobtainable, the chef will use the Horn of Plenty to set off patés and terrines. Dried and powdered they make a useful condiment for flavoring stews.

Bottom right on the opposite page is the cap of a Horn of Plenty seen from above. Some specimens have a lacy look as this one does.

THE GRAY OR EARTHY AGARIC

Tricholoma terreum

We could say that the Earthy Agaric is one of those mushrooms handicapped by an unfortunate name; after all the adjective *earthy* does nothing to help its personality. But, as so often happens, appearances are deceptive, and in addition the color is more reminiscent of a pretty fur coat than muddy earth.

Cap	Dark gray becoming lighter as the mushroom develops, fragile, cone-shaped then flattened out, umbonate, covered with fine silky streaks. 1 to 3 inches across.
Gills	Emarginate, unequal, light gray.
Spores	Yellowish-white.
Stem	Grayish-white, fibrous and silky, cylindrical, tall. Neither volva nor ring.
Habitat	Woods, clearings. Often under pines.
Season	Fall.
Special Features	This is a mushroom one finds late in the season and can only be confused with the poisonous Tiger Tricholoma *(Tricholoma pardinum)*, which is of a stockier build and is more clearly marked with streaks on the cap.

Note	EARTHY AGARIC	TIGER TRICHOLOMA
Color	Gray.	Blackish-brown or blackish-gray.
Cap	Flat, umbonate in center.	Convex, thick, humped.
Stem	Long, slender, grayish-white.	Short, thick, brownish.

Recipes	The Earthy Agaric has a subtle taste. It is easily preserved, which is convenient when winter is not far away and mushrooms of all kinds are becoming scarce. Dried, it can be used later on in Chinese cookery which often requires perfumed mushrooms. More simply, serve it with stews and pickled meats to bring out their country flavor.

This mushroom often comes up in large numbers growing close together, so it is easy to pick a lot in a short time. But please do not pick more than you need because this over-picking causes needless destruction.

Fear of poisonous mushrooms often approaches superstition. Even if they are dangerous they cause fewer deaths than those re-nown killers—dangerous drivers. A person who draws back in horror from a plate of mushrooms will not hesitate to sit next to a driver who is careless or, worse, drunk!

Occasionally a classic author has indulged in questionable humor about poisonous mushrooms. Sacha Guitry begins his novel *The Tale of a Cheat* with the sentence, "I was orphaned by a meal of mushrooms."

THE PEZIZAS

Peziza auranta   *Peziza onotica*

These pretty little orange or buff-colored bowls come in complicated shapes. They grow right down on the ground with a short stalk thrust into the humus. There is no possibility of mistaking them. They appear in woods in the fall.

Recipes   The Orange Fairy Cup Peziza or Orange Peel Peziza *(Peziza auranta)* is one of the very few mushrooms that can be eaten raw. It is prudent to cook nearly all mushrooms since some of them contain poisonous substances that are destroyed by heat. Pezizas can be dressed like a salad.

The Orange Ear Peziza *(Otidea onotica)*, or Hare's Ears, have thin, fragile flesh that shrinks in the cooking, so they are better put in an omelet or made into a sauce, but cook them in butter first to bring out the taste.

Peziza (Sarcoscypha) coccinea

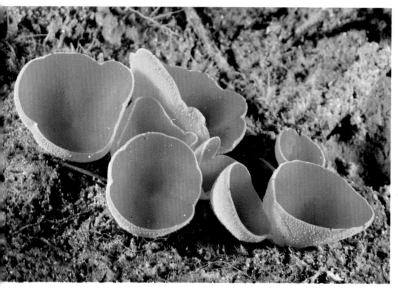

Above, Peziza aurantia; *below,* Peziza anotica

THE CORAL FUNGI

In the fall, woods are often full of these strange, little, bright-colored tufts of coral fungus. Some are slender and some stubby, but they are unmistakable. There is not a really poisonous one but some are too bitter and others are purgative, so stay with the three following kinds:

The Golden Coral *(Clavaria aurea):* Thick trunk, cream or yellowish-white, fairly thick branches finely forked and sharp pointed. Not to be confused with the Beautiful Clavaria *(Clavaria formosa)* which is more slender, has a pink trunk and branches with lemon-yellow tips. This one causes diarrhea.

The Purple-Tipped Coral *(Clavaria botrytes):* A thick, white trunk with yellowish branches finely divided into pink tips.

The Cup-Bearing Clavaria *(Clavaria cinerea):* Short trunk, whitish or pale gray. Branches gray, unequal in length.

Recipes   Clavaria are full of water, so cut them in pieces and put them in a pan without any fat and heat quickly until all the water has evaporated, then brown them in butter. Preserved in vinegar in the same way as gherkins they make an excellent pickle to eat with cold meat.

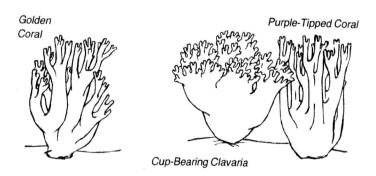

Golden Coral

Purple-Tipped Coral

Cup-Bearing Clavaria

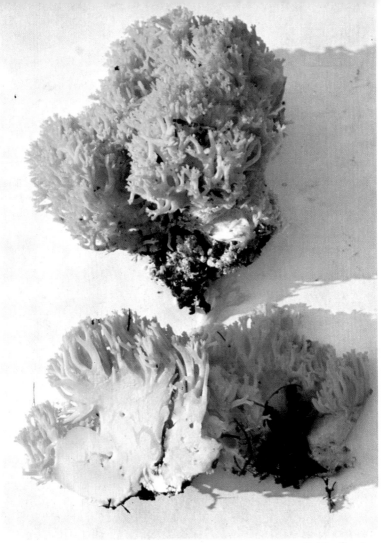

Golden Coral

Believe it or not—there are people who actually intoxicate them-selves deliberately by swallowing poisonous mushrooms without any thought of suicide. The explanation is that any discomfort lasts only for an hour or two and they derive some kind of satisfaction from it. This is practiced in Asia where the juice is extracted from the Fly Amanita and used for getting drunk.

To be fair we must admit that grape juice, which is quite harmless can also be a poison and we show every indulgence toward those who drink too much of it.

THE BLUELEG

Tricholoma saevus

Conoisseurs of the Blueleg prefer it to its close relative the Wood Blewit (see page 82).

Cap	Convex, then flattened, fleshy, chamois-colored or pale buff sometimes tinted with mauve. 2½ to 5 inches across.
Gills	Crowded, unequal, whitish, slightly emarginate.
Spores	Pinkish-gray.
Stem	Sturdy, short, firm, cylindrical, sometimes swollen at the base, whitish, covered with mauve fibrils. Neither volva nor ring.
Habitat	Fields.
Season	Fall.
Special Features	The mauve-colored fibrils on the stem prevent it from being mistaken for anything similar.
Recipes	The best way to cook this excellent mushroom is in oil, butter, or bacon fat, with aromatic herbs and finely chopped shallots.

Mushrooms are mysterious creatures. Nobody can predict with any certainty where they will come up and, although we may set off full of confidence for the spot where we found them last year, we are often disappointed. Throughout history they have haunted the imagination of mankind, inspiring fear and admiration at the same time and many legends have grown up around them. One gives a delightful account of how mushrooms first appeared.

Christ and St. Peter were traveling together and asked for food when they came to a village. The villagers gave them both white bread and brown bread, and, going on their way, they passed through a forest eating their lunch and letting fall a few crumbs. Where the white bread fell, edible mushrooms sprang up, but the brown crumbs brought forth poisonous ones.

Learned botanists can give us much more precise explanations, but somehow the poetic note is missing.

THE WOOD BLEWIT

Lepista (Tricholoma) nuda

A handsome, lilac-colored mushroom that is rarely attacked by insects. Perhaps it is protected by its smell, which is pleasant but hard to define.

Cap	Convex then flattened, violet-colored at first, becoming brownish. 2½ to 5 inches across.
Gills	Crowded, unequal, emarginate, adnate. Violet at first, brownish later.
Spores	Pinkish-beige.
Stem	Cylindrical, swollen at the base, firm, lilac-colored. Neither volva or ring.
Habitat	Pinewoods, sometimes deciduous woods.
Season	Fall, occasionally winter.
Special Features	Always the same color. Can only be confused with other violet-colored mushrooms, which are also edible.
Recipes	Cooking in butter retains the subtle perfume of this highly prized mushroom. It can be put in with roasts and stews too.

The Wood Blewit is one of the mushrooms that respond to cultivation, and specialists in France have grown them in the vaults of the Paris Observatory. However, professional growers do not pay as much attention to this species as to the ordinary Button Mushroom. They probably think that a public used to the familiar "mushroom" would not take kindly to a lilac-colored one.

*

There are mushrooms that cannot be classified as edible because they are either tasteless or frankly dangerous; but, nevertheless, when given suitable treatment they have their uses. The enormous

value of penicillin cannot be calculated. The mold from which penicillin is extracted belongs to the family of mushrooms. Less well known is the use made of the ergot found on rye, the little, black crescent-shaped parasite that grows on the ears of cereals and grasses. Ground up with flour and made into bread, ergot has often caused accidents. In the Middle Ages, ergot was the cause of burning pains that reached epidemic proportions and they were known as "St. Anthony's Fire." Even today it is not unknown for a batch of bread to be infected, but fortunately that is rare indeed. Ergot of rye can cause serious trouble but it also provides a medicament that is extremely useful for the treatment of certain conditions—the substance called ergotine.

THE GRAYCAP
or MIST FUNGUS

Clitocybe nebularis

Perhaps they take their name from their shaded gray color, which is darker toward the center, or is it from the tufts they so often form? Your basket will be full if you find them when the conditions of temperature and humidity are just right.

Cap	Pale gray at the edges, darker toward the center, with a powdery look. Rounded then flattened, finally bowl-shaped. Margin curves inward when young. 2 to 8 inches across. Smells of fresh flour.
Gills	Crowded, adnate-decurrent, unequal, whitish.
Spores	White.
Stem	Strong, slender, swollen at the base, whitish, firm then hollow. Neither volva nor ring.
Habitat	Woods, or partly wooded places. Grows in circles or in lines.
Season	Fall. This is one of the last mushrooms of the season and it makes a welcome appearance when the first frosts begin during the first two weeks of November.
Special Features	It must be distinguished from the Livid Entoloma *(Entoloma lividum)*, which is extremely poisonous:

Note	GRAYCAP	LIVID ENTOLOMA
Gills	Adnate, decurrent. Whitish.	**Pink** when fully grown, but yellowish when young.
Spores	White.	Pink.

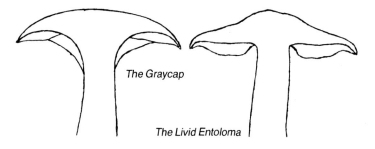

The Graycap

The Livid Entoloma

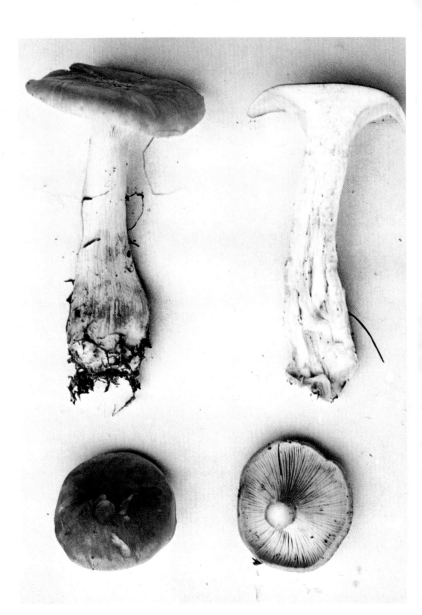

Recipes　　Not easily digested, it should be blanched first. It can then be put into game stews and other meat served in gravy.

AMANITA PHALLOIDES

deadly

THE DEATH CAP

Amanita phalloides

Although this is a book about edible mushrooms, we have made an exception in the case of one or two poisonous ones that must be known so that they can be avoided. This is especially the case with the terrible *Amanita phalloides*, which is responsible for nearly every case of fatal poisoning.

Amanita phalloides, the Death Cap, is not the only one of its kind in being so dangerous; the Destroying Angel *(Amanita virosa)* and the Spring Amanita *(Amanita verna)* are just as relentless, although fortunately they are much rarer. These last two mushrooms have the same features as the Death Cap—the same shaped cap, same gills, and same stem with ring and volva. The only difference is in the color of the cap. The cap of *Amanita phalloides* is greenish varying in shade, but the caps of *Amanita virosa* and *Amanita verna* are entirely white.

There are some commonly held beliefs about so-called tests for recognizing edible mushrooms. One is that insects and grubs eat only good ones. This is absolutely false and could lead to disaster in the case of *Amanita phalloides*, which is frequently eaten by slugs. The human digestive system is not the same as that of all members of the animal kingdom and what can be eaten by some animals may be fatal to others.

Prejudice persists concerning other so-called tests; for instance, one belief is that if the flesh turns blue it is a poisonous mushroom. This is not an indication of poison and many excellent boleti turn blue, whereas the flesh of the Death Cap always stays white.

False too is the belief that a silver coin will turn black if put in a pot with a poisonous mushroom. Fortunately silver coins are rare these days so this worthless experiment is not so easy to carry out.

The Amanita phalloides *can retain all its essential characteristics (color of gills, ring, volva) and yet appear in different guises.*
The photograph on the left and the one on the next page illustrate possible variations.

THE DEATH CAP

(continued)

Cap	Olive green, varying in intensity, striated with black fibers running to the margin; silky, slimy when wet, breaks out of a white egg when it comes up through the soil, then becomes domed or slightly conical and finally flattened. 2 to 4 inches across.
Gills	**White,** unequal.
Spores	**White.**
Stem	Slender, firm then hollow, whitish, swollen at the base into a volva. **Skirt-shaped ring. Volva.**
Habitat	Woods.
Season	Summer, fall.
Special Features	**Deadly poisonous.** Its poison goes deep into the organs of the body without first producing any feeling of illness. The same can be said of the two other varieties already mentioned:

> Destroying Angel *(Amanita virosa),* which is white.
> Spring Amanita *(Amanita verna),* which is white.

Throw out any mushroom that combines all the following features:

Cap	**WHITE OR GREENISH, OLIVE GREEN.**
Gills	**WHITE.**
Spores	**WHITE.**
Stem	**WITH VOLVA AND RING.**

Note: There are some edible kinds with all these features but beginners should ignore these until they become more experienced.

Amanita phalloides,
deadly

LATIN NAMES AND POPULAR NAMES

The scientific world has given mushrooms Latin names to avoid mistakes when translating from one language to another. However the specialists do not always agree among themselves about their correct attribution, and their opinions are occasionally modified by later discoveries. For instance the Meadow Mushroom began life as an *Agaric* before turning into a *Psalliota* and finally becoming *Pratella*.

What can we say then about the country names people give them and which are highly local in use? There are hundreds of them and a few that refer to color or appearance have spread far and wide. We quote one or two of the more picturesque ones:

Toadstools, Toads' Hats, Poddockstools

Horse Mushrooms, Snowballs

Shaggy Mane, Inky Cap

Horn of Plenty, Cornucopia, Trumpet of Death

Parasols, Drumsticks

Fairy Ring Mushroom, Scotch Bonnets

Spreading-Hedgehog, Sheep's foot.

It happens that the same local name is applied to several quite different species of mushrooms, according to where you are, so for safety's sake we recommend that attention be paid only to the essential characteristics of a mushroom and to its Latin name.

BIBLIOGRAPHY

Atkinson, G.F. *Mushrooms, Edible, Poisonous, Etc.* New York: Hafner Publishing Co., reprint 1961.

Bigelow, Howard E. *The Mushroom Pocket Field Guide.* New York: Macmillan, 1974.

Christensen, Clyde M. *Common Edible Mushrooms.* Minneapolis: University of Minnesota Press, 1970.

Krieger, Louis C. *The Mushroom Handbook.* New York: Dover Publications, reprint 1967.

Lange M., and F.B. Hora. *A Guide to Mushrooms and Toadstools.* New York: E.P. Dutton and Co., 1967.

McIlvaine, C., and R.K. Macadam. *One Thousand American Fungi.* Indianapolis: Bobbs-Merrill, 1912. Reprint 1973, Dover Publications.

McKenny, Margaret. *Savory Wild Mushroom.* Seattle: University of Washington Press, 1971.

Rinaldi, Augusto and Tynaldo, Vassili. *The Complete Book of Mushrooms.* New York: Crown Publishers, Inc., 1972.

Smith, Alex H. *Mushroom Hunter's Field Guide.* Ann Arbor: University of Michigan Press, 1974.

Thomas, W.S. *Field Book of Common Mushrooms.* New York: G.P. Putnam's Sons, 1948.

PHOTOGRAPHIC CREDITS

Y. Lanceau, pp. 43, 51; P. Joly, pp. 32 botton, 77 bottom; H. Schrempp, pp. 37 top, 38 bottom; J. Six, pp. 41, 59, 76 top; V. Waldvogel, pp. 21, 23, 25, 31, 33, 39, 53, 55, 59 bottom, 63, 68, 69, 71 top, 73 bottom, 81, 89.

The photographs on pages 27, 29, 35, 36, 45, 47, 49, 56, 57, 61, 65, 66, 67, 71 bottom, 73 top, 75, 77 top, 79, 83, 85, 86 have kindly been supplied by the author, who took them with the help of A. Voye.

INDEX OF LATIN AND POPULAR NAMES

(page numbers in italics indicate color plate)

INDEX OF LATIN AND POPULAR NAMES

(page numbers in italics indicate color plate)

books on art

An exciting series of books dealing with fine art and graphic design. Each volume is copiously illustrated with full-color reproductions of paintings, drawings, and original designs suitable for framing.

The Painter and the Man
12"x12", clothbound, boxed
- BONNARD, $59.95
- BOSCH, $69.95
- BRUEGHEL, $59.95
- CEZANNE, $59.95
- EL GRECO, $59.95
- GAUGUIN, $59.95
- MONET, $59.95
- VAN GOGH, $59.95
- VERMEER, $59.95

Artist's Series
9⅜"x9¼"
$10.95 paperbound

CEZANNE	JONGKIND	ROUAULT
COROT	LORRAIN	ROUSSEAU
DAUMIER	MICHELANGELO	RUBENS
DELACROIX	MILLET	SEURAT
DURER	MOREAU	TURNER
FRAGONARD	POUSSIN	VAN GOGH
GOYA	REMBRANDT	WATTEAU

Artist's Watercolor Series, $29.95 each
COROT   FOUQUET   GUARDI

DEATH OF A TREE by Folon. 11"x14", $29.95 paperbound.
LETTRES A GIORGIO by Folon; some in collaboration with Milton Glaser, Roy Lichtenstein, others. 4⁵⁄₁₆"x9⁵⁄₁₆", $14.95 paperbound.
ART NOUVEAU by B. Champigneulle. The movement in architecture, decorative arts, painting, graphics. 6"x9", $10.95 paper, $13.95 cloth.

French Provincial Cuisine Christian Délu

A new cookbook with over 240 recipes and 180 full-color photographs. Includes specialties of various regions, with easy-to-follow recipes for appetizers, soups, vegetables, fish and shellfish, meats, salads, poultry and game and desserts. $15.95 clothbound.

Lenôtre's Desserts and Pastries

Lenôtre, France's famous pastry chef
Duplicate the pastry accomplishments of France's leading pastry house, with step-by-step procedures for making puff pastries, meringues, eclairs, brioche, and many other delights. $16.95 clothbound.

Le Répertoire de La Cuisine Louis Saulnier

The classic reference to French culinary terms used by restaurateurs for years. Explains the ingredients for all classic French dishes. For the amateur as well as the professional.
$6.95 cloth, standard edition; $10.95 cloth, deluxe edition

Great Ideas for Planning, Cooking, and Serving

Brunch Pauline Durand, Yolande Languirand

Over 100 quick, easy-to-prepare recipes for patés, souffles, hearty meat dishes, casseroles, breads, salads and boozy desserts. Tips on ahead-of-time preparation, menus, and serving with flair. $2.50 paperbound.

Chinese Cooking Ayako Namba

Regional specialties, with suggestions on selecting and preparing the dishes, serving customs, proper utensils, and so forth. $3.95 paperbound.